STORIES
THAT
JESUS CHRIST
TOLD

with reflective meditations

CLAIRE-LOUISE BAKER

Copyright © 2014 by Claire-Louise Baker

Stories that Jesus Christ told
with reflective meditations
by Claire-Louise Baker

Printed in the United States of America

ISBN 9781498401456

All rights reserved solely by the author. The author guarantees all contents are original and do not infringe upon the legal rights of any other person or work. No part of this book may be reproduced in any form without the permission of the author. The views expressed in this book are not necessarily those of the publisher.

Scripture quotations taken from The Kingdom Interlinear Translation of the Greek Scriptures. Copyright © 1985 by New World Bible Translation Committe.

www.xulonpress.com

INTRODUCTION

A historic tradition of using moral stories to illustrate spiritual teachings exists in Judaism. Rabbis have always used parables to define profound principles. Christ continued this tradition as he traveled around the cities and villages of Israel. The imagery and situations used are familiar to the environment of the Jewish and Greco-Roman culture of that time, over two thousand years ago.

A collection of parables from Christ's teachings are re-told here and coherently linked together in connection with the first part of his Sermon on the Mount. Following each one is a reflective meditation which positively affirms our ability to do the Will of our Father.

TABLE OF CONTENTS

9. . . . . .The Sower and the Seed
12. . . . . .The Barren Fig Tree
15. . . . . The Rich Fool
18. .The Cunning Manager

22. . . . . The Widow and the Reluctant Judge

26. . . . . The Pharisee and the Tax Collector
29. . . . . The Investors
33. . . . . .The Useless Servant
36. . . . . The Wedding Guest

40. . . . . The Prodigal Son
45. . . . . .The Great Banquet
49. . . . . A Friend at Midnight
52. . . . . The Hardworking Servant

56. . . . . .The Creditor and his Debtors
59 . .The Merciful King and his Unforgiving Servant
63. . . . . The Good Samaritan
66. . . . . The Rich Man and Lazarus

71.	The Fruitful Tree
74.	The Lost Sheep
77.	A Rafter in the Eye
80.	The Lost Coin
83.	The Lamp of the Body
86.	The Lamp Stand
89.	The Faithful and Wise Servants
93.	The Workers in the Vineyard
97.	The Two Sons
100.	Building a Tower
103.	A King Sues for Peace
107.	The Bad Tenants

Teacher, what good shall I do in order that I might have everlasting life?
You shall not murder.
You shall not commit adultery.
You shall not steal.
You shall not bear false witness.
Be honouring your father and mother
and you shall Love your neighbour as yourself.

Matthew ~ chapter 19 verse 16

I am giving a new commandment to you that you Love one another as I have loved you.

John ~ chapter 13 verse 34

*Happy are those in need of
spiritual riches, they belong to
The Kingdom of Heaven*

Matthew ~ chapter 5 verse 3

THE SOWER AND THE SEED

Matthew ~ chapter 13 verse 3
Mark ~ chapter 4 verse 2
Luke ~ chapter 8 verse 5

A man was scattering seed and as he walked along some of the seed fell beside the way and having flown down, the birds ate them. Other seed fell on the rocky ground where there was not much soil and it immediately sprang up because of not having depth of soil. It was scorched as the sun rose and because of it having not taken root, it dried up. Others fell on the thorns and the thorns came up and choked them. But others still fell on the fine soil and it yielded fruit, some a hundred-fold, some sixty, some thirty.

The Word of God's Kingdom,
received in our minds,
is accepted by our joyful hearts.
Truth takes root
in the fine soil of the soul
where it will not pass away.
Living steadfastly in hope,
the disturbing ways of the world
will not cause our lives
to be a fruitless struggle.
Deep inner peace
is mindfully maintained
where the manifestation
of abundant virtue is cultivated.
Shaped by His amazing Grace,
a truly wholesome life
glorifies our Creator.
Aware of our spiritual needs,
we are happy to belong
in The Kingdom of Heaven.

Thorns and traps are in the way of the crooked one; he that is guarding his soul keeps well away from them.

King Solomon ~ Proverb 22 verse 5

Let those with ears hear.

Matthew ~ chapter 13 verse 9

THE BARREN FIG TREE

Luke ~ chapter 13 verse 6

A man had a fig tree planted in his vineyard but when he came to look for fruit in it he did not find any. He said to the vinedresser, "Look, for three years now I have been coming to look for figs on this tree and have not found any. Cut it down, it's a waste of space."

"Lord," the vinedresser replied, "Leave it there for one more year, I will turn the soil over and fertilize it, then it should make fruit but if not, then you could cut it out."

Idle ignorance
leads to a lack of Wisdom
but inspired and motivated,
we become what we were called to be.
The richness
of spiritual growth and development
is experienced
as our minds are nourished
with knowledge and understanding.
An inner transformation takes place
when a rejuvenated heart
is spiritually empowered with Love.
Yielding the fruits of virtue
we display true human flourishing.
Aware of our spiritual needs
we are happy to belong
in The Kingdom of Heaven.

Honour Jehovah with your valuable things and with the first fruits of all your produce.

King Solomon ~ Proverb 3 verse 9

My food is that I do the Will of the One having sent me.

John ~ chapter 4 verse 34

THE RICH FOOL

Luke ~ chapter 12 verse 16

The land belonging to a rich man produced such a good harvest that he didn't have enough space to keep it all. Reasoning within himself he said, 'What must I do now I have nowhere to gather my crops?!' So he said, 'I will do this; I will knock down my store-houses and build bigger ones to keep all my wheat and goods in and I will say to my soul, soul, you have plenty of good things stored up for many years to come; take life easy, eat, drink and enjoy your well-being.' But God said to him, "Senseless one, this night they are demanding your soul from you, but who then is to have the things you have prepared?"

The voice of the ego may lead us
to self-centered pride and greediness.
Using our conscience
we develop sound reasoning powers.
Life is not made secure
by the possession of worldly goods
and a lack of moral values
brings a sense of worthlessness.
Bountiful blessings
from our Heavenly Provider
are purposely used to serve Him.
Without attachment
to material wealth
we are giving towards the disadvantaged.
To be enriched with many good qualities
is recognised and rewarded by God.
Aware of our spiritual needs
we are happy to belong
in The Kingdom of Heaven.

Out of the heart's abundance the mouth speaks.

Matthew ~ chapter 12 verse 34
Luke ~ chapter 6 verse 45

A man's life is not secured by what he owns, even when he has more than he needs.

Luke ~ chapter 12 verse 15

THE CUNNING MANAGER

Luke ~ chapter 16 verse 1

A rich man had a steward who managed his business but was rumoured to be handling goods wastefully. So he said to him, "What is this I am hearing about you? Give back the accounts of your stewardship as you are not yet able to be steward." The steward said to himself, 'What shall I do now my Lord will take my stewardship from me? I am not strong enough to be digging, I am ashamed to beg; I know what I will do, in order that whenever I am to be transferred out of the stewardship they might receive me into their houses'.

And having called on each one of his Lord's loan-owners he said to the first one, "How much do you owe my Lord?" He replied, "One hundredth bath measures of olive oil." The steward said to him, "Take your written agreement and sit down quickly and write fifty." Then he said to another of his masters' debtors, "How much are you owing?" He replied, "One hundred measures of wheat." The steward said to him, "Have your written agreement and write eighty."

Acting upon immoral
and unreasonable thought
would foolishly lead us towards
deceitful and dishonourable ways.
Each held accountable for our actions,
we consequently earn respect
when living by our spiritual values.
God's credible people of principle
are reputed for having ethical integrity.
Being entrusted
with a role of responsibility
allows us to prove our worth
as trustworthy individuals.
The blessing of belonging
with our all-knowing Lord
is worth more than anything in the world.
Aware of our spiritual needs
we are happy to belong
in The Kingdom of Heaven.

God is for us a refuge and strength, a help that is present in times of trouble.

Psalm 46 verse 1

You cannot be servants to God and to money.

Matthew ~ chapter 6 verse 24
Luke ~ chapter 16 verse 13

*Happy are those in mourning,
they will be consoled.*

Matthew ~ chapter 5 verse 4

THE WIDOW AND THE RELUCTANT JUDGE

Luke ~ chapter 18 verse 1

A judge in the city was not God fearing or respectful of men. But there was a widow in that city who kept on approaching him saying, "Grant me justice from my adversary." He was not willing for some time, but after a while he said to himself, 'Although I am not God fearing nor do I respect man, because of the trouble this widow is giving me, I shall exact justice for her in order that she does not get to me in the end!'

Our wise and powerful God
does not favour the unjust.
Reverently we appeal
for His Law to be honoured on Earth
as it is in Heaven.
With faith we trust
in His solace and strength
in response to lonely cries of grief.
Feelings of sorrow and helplessness
during times of despair
are soothed and calmed
by God's restoring Grace.
Sympathetic condolences
comfort the bereaved
whose loved ones are sorely missed.
Those in mourning
are happy that they are consoled.

Conduct my case O Yahweh, against my opponents.

King David ~ Psalm 35 verse 1

Let Your loving kindness serve, please to comfort me.

Psalm 119 verse 76

Happy are those who die in union with the Lord from this time onward. Yes says the spirit, let them rest from their labours, for the good deeds they did go with them.

Revelations chapter 14 verse 13

God will be with them, and He will wipe every tear out of their eyes.

Revelations chapter 21 verse 4

Happy are the mild-tempered, they will inherit the Earth

Matthew ~ chapter 5 verse 5

THE PHARISEE AND THE TAX COLLECTOR

Luke ~ chapter 18 verse 9

Two men went up into a temple to pray, one a Pharisee the other a tax collector. The Pharisee stood and was praying, "God, I am thanking You because I am not on the same level as the rest of men, extortionists, unrighteous, adulterers, or also like this tax collector; I fast twice on the Sabbath, I give a tenth of all I acquire." However, the tax collector from a long way off, without having stood up was not willing to lift his eyes up towards heaven and was beating his breast saying, "God, let me the sinner reconcile with You."

Conceited arrogance
and obnoxious pride
creates an attitude of superiority
towards other people
and Almighty God.
His worshippers are not hypocrites
who boast about acts of kindness
whilst reproaching others
and seeking self-glorification.
Acknowledging our own faults,
we remorsefully ask for redemption
in the hope of living more virtuously.
With compassionate humility
our God is glorified.
His meek people are happy
that they will inherit the Earth.

When you go making gifts of mercy, do not blow a trumpet ahead of you just as the hypocrites do in the synagogues and in the streets so that they might be glorified by men.

Matthew ~ chapter 6 verse 2

And this is the confidence that we have towards him, that if ever we ask in accordance to His Will, He hears us.

1 John ~ chapter 5 verse 14

THE INVESTORS

Matthew ~ chapter 25 verse 14
Luke ~ chapter 19 verse 12

A noble man was about to go abroad to secure kingly power for himself. He called upon ten of his servants and gave them money, telling them to do business in the time he was away. The Lord returned having received the kingdom and summoned the servants to come and tell him what they had gained by trading. The first servant approached him saying, "Lord, your ten mina doubled itself." He said to them, "Well done indeed, good servant, because you proved to be faithful in the smallest matter you have authority over ten cities." Then the second servant came saying, "Your mina made five minas." He said to this one, "You will also be in charge of five cities." The next servant came along saying, "Lord, look! The mina of yours which I have lies in a sweat cloth; I was in fear of you because you are a harsh man; you take what you do not deposit and you reap what you have not sowed." His Lord answered, "Out of your own mouth I am judging you a wicked and sluggish servant. You knew that I am a harsh man, taking what I had not deposited and reaping what I did not sow? It was necessary for you therefore to throw the silver pieces of mine to the bankers and having come back I would have likely taken my money back with interest." So he said to those standing by, "Take the sum of money from him and give it to the one who has ten minas." They said, "Lord, he is being given ten minas."

With faith in God's Will,
a spirit of rebellion
will not distract us
from using our gifts and abilities
to invest in a hopeful future.
As worthy servants,
inspired to do good works,
we make worthwhile contributions
towards multiplying the wealth
of God's Kingdom.
Efforts and achievements
made in His honour
are rewarded accordingly;
with providence and abundant blessings.
His meek people are happy
that they will inherit the Earth.

To everyone that has, more will be given and he will have abundance; but as for him that does not have, even what he has will be taken away.

Matthew ~ chapter 25 verse 29

A servant is not greater than his Lord.

John ~ chapter 13 verse 16

THE USELESS SERVANT

Matthew ~ chapter 24 verse 45
Luke ~ chapter 12 verse 42

The servant whose Lord finds him giving the staff their measure of grain when it is due as he was appointed to do, will be happy. His Lord will entrust him with all of his belongings. But if an evil servant says in his heart, "My Lord is taking time to come back," and starts to beat his fellow servants and eat and drink with those getting drunk, the Lord of that servant will arrive on a day which he is not expecting, at a time which he does not know and will separate him and put him with the unfaithful hypocrites.

God's loyal servants
do not abuse others
or perpetrate cruel suffering
with acts of intimidation or aggression.
Practising the orderly principles
of compassion and kindness,
Truth and decency is conveyed,
not falsehood or wickedness.
Irrational, volatile behaviour
is prevented with patience and self-control.
Our solidarity is strengthened
as we do the Will of our Master
and seek protection
from the corrupt influence of Satan.
His meek people are happy
that they will inherit the Earth.

Happy is the man that has not walked in the counsel of the wicked ones, and in the way of sinners has not stood.

Psalm 1 verse 1

You are not fearful, little flock, because your Father thought well of you to be given the Kingdom.

Luke ~ chapter 12 verse 32

THE WEDDING GUEST

Luke ~ chapter 14 verse 7

Whenever you may be called by someone into wedding festivities, you should not take the best place to sit because somebody more honourable than you may then be called in by him too, and the one who invited you both will say to you, "Give your place to this person." Then you will have to move with shame to the worst seat. But whenever you have been called and then gone into a feast, quickly take the worst seat in order that whenever the one who invited you might come over, he will say to you, "Friend, move up towards the top." Then glory will be given to you in sight of all those sitting with you.

The call from our kind God
to come to celebrate
life in His Kingdom
is humbly responded to
without conceited arrogance.
Our willingness
to behave courteously
is displayed with
actions of modest selflessness.
A sense of community is enjoyed
by His friendly and fortunate people.
With consideration and respect
for each other,
gratitude is shown
for God's gracious favour.
His meek people are happy
that they will inherit the Earth.

I, Yahweh am your God, the One teaching you to benefit yourself, the One causing you to tread in the way in which you should walk.

Isaiah ~ chapter 48 verse 17

I am mild tempered and humble in heart, you will find refreshment for your souls.

Matthew ~ chapter 11 verse 28

*Happy are those hungering
and thirsting for justice,
they will be satisfied.*

Matthew ~ chapter 5 verse 6

THE PRODIGAL SON

Luke ~ chapter 15 verse 1

A man had two sons and the younger of them said to the father, "Father, give me the part of the property that falls to be my share." But he divided the means of living and gave it to them. And after having spent not many days together doing everything which needed to be done, the younger son traveled abroad into a country far away and there he squandered what he had, living as a wasteful spender. Having spent all that he had there came to be a severe famine in that far away country and he started to be in need. He actually went and attached himself to one of the citizens of that country who sent him into his fields to feed pigs. He desired to satisfy his hunger with what the pigs were eating and no one was giving towards him. Having come to his senses he said, "How many of my fathers hired men have and abundance of bread, but there is a famine here, I am perishing, when I get up I shall go towards my father and I shall say to him, "Father, I sinned in front of heaven and in sight of you, I am not yet worthy to be called your son; make me like one of the hired men of yours." And having risen he came towards his father.

But while he had a long way yet to go, his father saw him and was moved with pity and having run, he fell upon his neck and kissed him. But the son said to the father, "I sinned in front of heaven and in sight of you; I am not yet worthy to be called your son. Make me one of your hired men." The father said to his servants, "Quick! Bring out the best robe and clothe him, put a ring on his hand and sandals on his feet and bring the wheat-fed calf to be sacrificed and having eaten let us be at ease, because this son of mine was dead and he came to life again, he had been lost and was found." And they started to feel at ease.

But his older son was in the field and as he was coming nearer to the house he heard dance music and having called towards him some of the servants, he was inquiring about what the reason for it was; one said to him, "Your brother has arrived, and your father sacrificed the wheat-fed calf because he received him back in good health." But he became wrathful and was not willing to enter. His father came out and started pleading with him. In reply he said to his father, "For so many years I have served you and never once transgressed your commands and yet not once did you ever give me even a kid for me to enjoy myself with my friends. But as soon as this son of yours who used up your means of living with harlots arrived, you slaughtered the fattened young bull for him." Then he said to him, "Child, you have always been with me, and what is mine is yours; but we just had to enjoy ourselves and rejoice because this brother of yours was dead and came to life, he was lost and then found."

To foolishly pursue
our ego's curious desires
would jeopardise
our close relationship with God.
Those who feel regret
after rebelling against
our wise Father
can find salvation
by striving to live differently
in His healing presence.
Embracing life with God
effectively ensures the development
of our spiritual maturity.
Free from resentment or envy,
His beloved children value one another
and pray for those
who are distant from Him.
We are happy
that our hunger and thirst
for righteousness will be satisfied.

My flesh has grown faint with longing for you in a land dry and exhausted where there is no water.

King David ~ Psalm 63 verse 1

The one saying he is in the light whilst hating his brother is still in the dark.

1 John ~ chapter 2 verse 9

THE GREAT BANQUET

Matthew ~ chapter 22 verse 1
Luke ~ chapter 14 verse 16

A king had prepared marriage festivities for his son. He sent his servants off to call those invited into the marriage festivities but they were not willing to come. Again he sent other servants off saying, "Say to those invited, look! I have prepared my dinner, the bulls and the fattened animals have been slaughtered and everything is ready; come to the marriage festivities!"

But they did not care and went off, one to his own field and one to do his commercial business; but the others seized the king's servants, treated them with disrespect and killed them.

The king grew wrathful and having sent his armies, he destroyed the murderers and burned their city. Then he said to his servants; "The marriage feast is indeed ready, those invited were not worthy; therefore go to the side roads and invite as many as you can find to the marriage festivities." And having gone out into the side ways, those servants led together all of those who they found, wicked people as well as good people; and the wedding room was filled with people sitting in it.

The wonderful invitation
to come to celebrate and rejoice
with our Sovereign God
is gladly accepted
without concern for worldly gains.
Our hearts cannot be made content
with a materialistic mentality;
to greedily desire
temporary sensual pleasures
would tempt us away from Him.
Blessed with spiritual nourishment,
communing with God unites His people.
We are happy
that our hunger and thirst
for righteousness will be satisfied.

He took a loaf, gave thanks, broke it and gave it to them.

Luke ~ chapter 22 verse 19

If anyone is thirsty let him come to me and drink.

John ~ chapter 7 verse 37

A FRIEND AT MIDNIGHT

Luke ~ chapter 11 verse 5

Who would have a friend who comes to him at midnight saying, "Friend, lend me three loaves of bread as a friend of mine has just come from far away to my home and I do not have anything to place in front of him." And from inside answer, "Do not trouble me. Anyway the door has already been locked and my little children are in bed, I am not able to stand up to give it to you."

If he will not give it to him having stood up because he is his friend, then due to the fact of his lack of modesty; having got up he will give as many loaves as he is in need of.

We gratefully rely on God
to provide sustaining strength
on the journey through life.
He cares about our well-being
and listens when we come to Him
in heartfelt prayer.
His amazing Grace enables us
to be slow to frustration or anger
and to convey His qualities
of kindness and empathy.
When we ask for help
with serving others
Yahweh responds
with restoring benevolence.
We are happy
that our hunger and thirst
for righteousness will be satisfied.

Ask and it will be given to you, seek and you will find, knock and the door will be opened to you.

Matthew ~ chapter 7 verse 7

Anyone that does not Love has not come to God, because God is Love.

1 John ~ chapter 4 verse 8

THE HARDWORKING SERVANT

Luke ~ chapter 17 verse 7

A man whose servant had been ploughing or minding a flock of sheep and had just come in from the field would not say to him, "Come now and sit at the table alongside me." But would he not say, "Make what I will eat for supper and put on an apron and serve me until I might eat and drink and afterwards you will eat and drink"?

Realising our moral obligations
with selfless devotion
will make us
disciplined and dependable servants
of our Heavenly Master.
Depending on Him
to cater for our needs,
we continue to demonstrate our dedication
and resolve to serve Him
diligently with good deeds.
Abiding with God
whilst adhering to His Will
makes daily life
meaningful and rewarding.
We are happy
that our hunger and thirst
for righteousness will be satisfied.

Come to me, all you who are working laboriously and loaded down, I will refresh you.

Matthew ~ chapter 11 verse 28

Yahweh Himself gives strength to His people. Yahweh blesses His people with peace.

King David ~ Psalm 29 verse 11

*Happy are the merciful ones,
they will be shown mercy*

Matthew ~ chapter 5 verse 7

THE CREDITOR AND HIS DEBTORS

Luke ~ chapter 7 verse 41

Two men were in debt to someone who had lent them money; one of them owed five hundred denarii and the other only fifty. Not being able to pay him back, the lender freely forgave both of them and the one who had more debt to be forgiven had the most love for him.

Burdened by our own
sinful transgressions,
we understand the need
for sanctifying forgiveness.
With thankful praise
for His compassionate blessings
of loving-kindness,
we are indebted to the Giver of Life.
His mercy keeps us at ease
and a peacefully clear mind glorifies Him.
Liberated by His Power,
we are free to focus
on practising virtuousness.
The merciful are happy
that they will be shown mercy.

Happy is the one who transgression is pardoned, whose sin is covered.

King David ~ Psalm 32 verse 1

Seven times daily I have praised You because of Your righteous rulings.

Psalm 119 verse 164

THE MERCIFUL KING AND HIS UNFORGIVING SERVANT

Matthew ~ chapter 18 verse 23

A king was willing to settle his accounts with his servants; he started the settling with one man who was led towards him who was in ten thousand talents of debt. But not being able to pay it back, his Lord commanded him to be sold as a slave with his wife and children and all his possessions so that his debt would be paid. The servant fell to his knees and was bowing towards him saying, "Be patient with me, I shall give back all that I owe." Moved with pity, the master of the servant forgave him the loan and let him go. Having gone out, the servant found one of his fellow servants who owed him one hundred denarii and having got hold of him was choking him saying, "Give back what you owe." His servant fell to his knees making an emotional request, saying, "Be patient with me and I will pay you back." But the servant was not willing to forgive him and had him thrown into prison until he could pay back the amount he owed. After witnessing this happening, his fellow servants complained a lot and having come to the master they reported to him what had occurred. His master summoned the servant towards him saying, "Wicked servant, I forgave you all your debt after you begged me to, was it not necessary for you also to have mercy on the fellow servant of yours?" And having been made wrathful, his master let him be tormented until he paid back all that he owed.

Repentant for our wrongdoings,
we plead for redemption
hoping to be pardoned with Love.
A clear conscience enables us
to obediently serve
our Sovereign God
in His Great Kingdom.
Freedom from sin saves us
from the burden of worry and guilt;
giving us a more positive
and patient temperament.
An ethical mentality
brings us to realise
our empathy for others.
The merciful are happy
that they will be shown mercy.

If you forgive men their trespasses, your heavenly Father will also forgive yours.

Matthew ~ chapter 6 verse 14

Be repentant for the Kingdom of the Heavens has drawn near.

Matthew ~ chapter 4 verse 17

THE GOOD SAMARITAN

Luke ~ chapter 10 verse 30

A man was going down from Jerusalem into Jericho and became a victim of robbers; having stripped him of his belongings and beaten him with many blows, they went off, leaving him almost dead.

Coincidently a Priest was going along that way and having seen him, went along on the other side. A Levite came down along the same way and having seen him he also went by on the opposite side. But a Samaritan came making his way down towards him and having seen him was moved with pity, and having reached him he bounded up his wounds, pouring on oil and wine. And after having mounted him upon his donkey, he led him to an inn and there he took care of him. In the morning he gave his two denarii to the innkeeper saying, "Take care of him, and in the likelihood that you might spend more I shall repay you when I come back in here."

Neighbourly and noble,
God's people do not follow
in the way of the mean spirited
who ignore the pain and suffering of others.
Without prejudice or discrimination,
we are moved by compassion
to come to the aid
of those experiencing trauma
due to the brutality of wrongdoers.
It is acknowledged and appreciated by God
when help is provided discretely
to vulnerable victims of violence.
The merciful are happy
that they will be shown mercy.

But I am afflicted and poor. Jehovah himself takes account of me.

King David ~ Psalm 40 verse 17

Having heard his parables the chief Priests and the Pharisees knew that he was talking about them.

Matthew ~ chapter 21 verse 45
Luke ~ chapter 16 verse 19

THE RICH MAN AND LAZARUS

A certain man was rich and clothed himself in purple linen and enjoyed a lavish and luxurious lifestyle from day to day. But a poor man named Lazarus had been put at his gate having been ulcerated and was desiring to satisfy his hunger from the scraps of food falling from the man's table, but the dogs were coming and licking his ulcers. It occurred that the poor man did die and he was to be carried off by angels into the bosom of Abraham. But the rich man also died and he was buried. In the Hades, having lifted up his eyes being in torment, he would see Abraham a long way off from him and Lazarus was held to his chest. He called and said, "Father Abraham, have mercy on me and send Lazarus in order that he might dip the tip of his finger in water and cool my tongue as this flame is causing me pain." But Abraham said, "Child, remember you took the good things of yours in your life and Lazarus received the bad; but now here he is being comforted but you are being pained. Anyway, with all this between us and you, a great chasm has been fixed so that those who are willing to step through from here towards you are not able to and neither may you cross over from there." He said, "But I am requesting therefore father, that you should send him to the house of my father, as I have five brothers and he may then thoroughly witness to them, in order that they might not come into this place of torment."

Abraham said, "They have Moses and the Prophets, let them hear of them." Then he said, "No, Father Abraham, if someone from the dead goes to them, they will repent." But he said, "If they have not listened and learned from Moses and from the Prophets, they won't be persuaded if a dead person stands up either."

The Power of God's Word saves us
from foolish gluttony,
superficial vanity
and hedonistic over indulgence.
Prosperity provides us
with a moral obligation
to give charitable donations
to the impoverished.
His fortunate people reach out
to help and comfort
the sick and the dying
so that they may retain their dignity
and know that God is loving and kind.
The merciful are happy
that they will be shown mercy.

Sell your belongings and give to the poor and you will have treasure in heaven.

Matthew ~ chapter 19 verse 21

For the one that does not practice mercy will have his judgment without mercy.

James ~ chapter 2 verse 13

*Happy are the pure in heart,
they will see God.*

Matthew ~ chapter 5 verse 8

THE FRUITFUL TREE

Matthew ~ chapter 7 verse 16
Luke ~ chapter 6 verse 43

From the fruits of men you will recognize them. They do not gather grapes from thorn bushes or figs from thistles. Every good tree produces fine fruit but the rotten tree produces bad fruit. A good tree is not able to bear bad fruit, neither is a rotten tree able to produce fine fruit. Every tree that is not able to produce fine fruit is cut down and thrown into the fire.

A good person brings good things out of the good treasure of the heart and the wicked person out of wickedness brings what is wicked; because out of the abundance of the heart, the mouth speaks.

Hopeless sinners are consumed
by poisonously impure thoughts
and harmful intentions
at the core of their being.
God knows the condition of our hearts;
motivated by His Love
we grow and mature
to express the manifestation
of His goodness.
The Power of Wisdom
creates pure, elevated thought
and a flourishing inner beauty
revealing a virtuous nature.
Moral values are upheld
and brought into fruition
by our speech and actions.
The pure in heart are happy
that they will see God.

How can you speak good things if you are evil?

Matthew ~ chapter 12 verse 34

Do not let your heart be troubled or afraid.

John ~ chapter 14 verse 27

THE LOST SHEEP

Matthew ~ chapter 18 verse 12
Luke ~ chapter 15 verse 4

Should a man who came to have one hundred sheep realize one of them had strayed, he would leave the ninety-nine upon the mountains having gone to search for the one straying. And if ever he might happen to find it, he would put it on his shoulders and rejoice over it more than the other ninety-nine having not strayed.

Losing sight of our Divine Protector
makes us vulnerable
to an attack from the enemy;
when peace of mind is lost
anxiousness takes hold.
Having trespassed away from Him,
we cry out to God in prayer
to be delivered from evil.
Seeking the right direction
we listen to His guidance,
knowing that Love is essence of His Word.
Angels celebrate
when the lost are found
and safe under God's watchful gaze,
fellowship is enjoyed.
The pure in heart are happy
that they will see God.

I have wandered like a lost sheep. O look for Your servant, for I have not forgotten Your commandments.

Psalm 119 verse 176

Yahweh is near to all those calling to Him, to all those who call upon him in trueness.

Psalm 145 of King David verse 18

I am the fine shepherd, the fine shepherd surrenders his soul for his sheep.

John ~ chapter 10 verse 11

A RAFTER IN THE EYE

Matthew ~ chapter 7 verse 3
Luke ~ chapter 6 verse 41

But why do you look at the sawdust in your brother's eye but not consider the rafter in your own eye? How can you say to your brother, "Let me take out the sawdust in your eye." When look! There is a rafter in your own eye?!

Aware of our need for mental purity,
judgmental and opinionated ways
are corrected with Wisdom
as we examine our thoughts.
For the Love of God
wrongful iniquities are discarded.
Without blindly dwelling
on the shortcomings of others
we consider our own faults.
Seeing the good in others
with a clear vision of peace,
we reflect Yahweh's Love.
The pure in heart are happy
that they will see God.

The way man sees is not the way God sees because mere man sees what appears to the eyes, but Yahweh sees what the heart is.

Samuel ~ chapter 16 verse 7

Search though me, O God and know my heart. Examine me and know my disquieting thoughts.

King David ~ Psalm 139 verse 23

THE LOST COIN

Luke ~ chapter 15 verse 8

Should a woman who has ten coins ever lose one coin, she would light a lamp and sweep the whole house carefully, looking to see if she could find it. After finding it she would call to her friends and neighbours saying, "Rejoice with me because I found the coin which I had lost."

Harbouring the shame
of guilt and regret
produces a dulled conscience
and bad state of mind.
Quietly looking within
to cleanse the souls inner chamber,
wasteful thinking patterns
and unwanted negativity
are consciously cleared away.
With the Power of God's forgiveness
tainted hearts are purified,
revived and refreshed.
The rediscovering
of treasured spiritual values
provides joyful delight.
The pure in heart are happy
that they will see God.

Create in me a pure heart O God.

King David ~ Psalm 51 verse 10

Your Word is a lamp to my foot, a Light on my path.

Psalm 119 verse 105

THE LAMP OF THE BODY

Matthew ~ chapter 6 verse 22
Luke ~ chapter 11 verse 34

The lamp of the body is your eye. Whenever your eye may be sound the whole of your body is enlightened; but whenever your eye is wicked, the whole of your body will also be dark.

Knowledge and understanding
of Truth and Wisdom
enlightens the mind's eye,
dispelling the darkness
of falsehood and ignorance.
The brilliance of God's Power is observed
as shadows of sinfulness
are removed from a repentant heart.
Joy and peace prevail
in the sacred sanctuary
of reflection and thought
where His illuminating Love shines.
The pure in heart are happy
that they will see God.

They have eyes full of adultery and are unable to desist from sin.

2 Peter ~ chapter 2 verse 14

The light has come into the world but men loved the darkness rather than the light as their works were wicked.

John ~ chapter 3 verse 19

THE LAMP STAND

Matthew ~ chapter 5 verse 14
Mark ~ chapter 4 verse 21
Luke ~ chapter 8 verse 16

Nobody after lighting a lamp puts it under a bowl, but instead they put it up on the lamp stand so it shines for all those in the house and those making their way in can see the light.

As the world around us
becomes dangerously dark
we walk profoundly,
without spiritual blindness
in the reassuring rays
of God's radiating Light.
Our souls shine
as a channel of His peace
when good deeds are seen
to bring Him glory.
His Love is like the warm golden glow
of a flame burning brightly in the night.
Those who feel lost and alone
may see the way forward
and change their outlook on life.
The pure in heart are happy
that they will see God.

You are the light of the world. A city is not able to be hidden when it lies on top of a mountain.

Matthew ~ chapter 5 verse 14

There is a lamp stand, all of it gold, with a bowl on top of it.

Zechariah ~ chapter 4 verse 2

THE FAITHFUL AND WISE SERVANTS

Luke ~ chapter 12 verse 36

Men waited for their Lord to arrive from marriages so that when he knocked they could immediately open the door to him. Those servants were happy when the Lord came and found them still awake; he would dress for service and have them recline at the table and then come alongside them and serve them!

And if on the second and third occasion they were found waiting, they would be happy for sure.

As vigilant and self-sacrificing
servants of God
we understand our honourable purpose
with mindful awareness.
Consciously looking beyond
the ego's physical cravings,
we patiently prepare to be of service
to our wonderful Lord.
The lamps of our hearts shine
with deep adoration for Him.
His Divine presence
is praised and glorified
as we receive His goodness
and enjoy a sense of well-being.
The pure in heart are happy
that they will see God.

Prepare to serve and let your lamps be burning.

Luke ~ chapter 12 verse 35

I am the light of the world. Those who follow me do not walk about in the darkness.

John ~ chapter 8 verse 12

*Happy are the peacemakers,
they will be called sons of God.*

Matthew ~ chapter 5 verse 9

THE WORKERS IN THE VINEYARD

Matthew ~ chapter 20 verse 1

A householder went out early one morning to hire workers to go into his vineyard; having agreed with the workers to pay them a denarius for the day, he sent them off into his vineyard.

Having gone out about three hours later he saw other unemployed men standing in the market and he said to them, "You also go and work in the vineyard, and whatever may be right I will give to you." They went away. Having gone out again about six and then nine hours later he did the same. But by about the eleventh hour, having gone out, he found others standing around and was saying to them, "Why were you standing here the whole day unemployed?" They were saying to him, "Because nobody hired us." He said to them, "Go and work in the vineyard as well." By the evening the lord of the vineyard said to the man in charge, "Call the workers and give them the wages, starting with the last ones until you get to the first ones." Those who had come about the eleventh hour individually received a denarius. Those who had come first thought they would receive more. However they also received one denarius each. Having received it they were muttering to the householder saying, "These ones worked for one hour, and you made them equals to us who have borne the burden of the day and the heat." He answered to one of them and said, "Fellow, I am not wronging you; did you not agree with me one denarius? Take what is yours and go; I am willing to give this last worker what I also give too you; am I not allowed to do what I want with what is mine? Or is your eye wicked because I am good?"

With free will we choose
to be obedient followers
of our Master's commands
and fulfill our highest potential
as His dutiful workers.
Trusting in Him
to keep His promises,
we know that God's Love
is shared equally among us.
Without being envious
of one another's blessings,
God's people of peace
gratefully accept His Way.
Peacemakers are happy to be
called God's children.

The mother and brothers of me are those hearing and doing the Word of God.

Luke ~ chapter 8 verse 21

You knew in the day what brought you towards peace – but now it is hidden from your eyes.

Luke ~ chapter 19 verse 42

THE TWO SONS

Matthew ~ chapter 21 verse 28

A man had two sons. Having gone towards the first one he said, "Child, go along today and work in the vineyard." Answering, his child said, "I will, Lord." But he did not go. Having gone towards the second one he said the same but this one answered, "I am not willing." But later, feeling regret, he went off to work.

Free from rebellious reluctance
or defiance,
we earnestly ensure
that God's Will is done.
The rewarding richness
of contentment
exists in our hearts
as we live in peace with Him.
With maturity and self-control
our time is spent wisely
behaving in a way that pleases
the Father of Creation.
Being compelled to do what is right
brings a meaningful sense of purpose.
Peacemakers are happy to be
called God's children.

Understand what sort of Love the Father has given us, in order that we should be called children of God.

1 John ~ chapter 3 verse 1

In that day you will know that I am in union with my Father and you are in union with me and I am in union with you.

John ~ chapter 14 verse 20

BUILDING A TOWER

Luke ~ chapter 14 verse 28

Who would be willing to build a tower without first sitting down and calculating the expense to see if he is able to complete it? Otherwise, at some point after having laid the foundations, he might not be capable of finishing it. And those seeing this might start to ridicule him saying, "This is the man who started building and was not able to finish!"

Trust in the future revelation
of God's Kingdom
is founded upon affirmed faith.
Without being discouraged
by mockery and ridicule,
a life wholly devoted
to our Heavenly Provider
is confidently invested in.
Realizing the potential
of our innate qualities,
the stability of our belief is proven.
We enjoy the security
of Divine protection and peace.
Peacemakers are happy to be
called God's children.

The name of Yahweh is a strong tower. Into it the virtuous run and are secure.

King Solomon ~ Proverb 18 verse 10

For you have proved to be a refuge for me, a strong tower against the enemy.

King David ~ Psalm 61 verse 3

A KING SUES FOR PEACE

Luke ~ chapter 14 verse 31

A king who is about to engage in war with another king will sit down first and take counsel to see if, with his ten thousand he will be able to go against the other kings' twenty thousand men. If it is not possible, then whilst still far away from him, he sends a body of ambassadors to make a request for peace between them.

The Supreme Commander
rules over our hearts and minds
as we pursue His Will on Earth.
Proceeding without compromise,
God's people move forward
in submissive solidarity;
boldly obeying His order
to strive for peace.
Free from living in fear
of hateful and oppressive tyrants,
we take refuge with our Sovereign God.
Our integral allegiance is affirmed
as we receive the shield
of His protection
and use the sword of His Word
to oppose the forces of evil.
Peacemakers are happy to be
called God's children.

Yahweh Himself will bless His people with peace.

King David ~ Psalm 29 verse 11

Do all you can to be peaceable.

Paul ~ letter to the Romans chapter 12 verse 18

Happy are those having been persecuted on account of righteousness, The Kingdom of Heaven is theirs.

Matthew ~ chapter 5 verse 10

THE BAD TENANTS

Matthew ~ chapter 21 verse 33

A man who was a householder planted a vineyard and put a fence around it; he dug a winepress and built a watch tower. He then let it out to cultivators before he traveled abroad. When the time drew near for the grapes to be ripe, he sent off the servants he had to collect his share of fruits. The cultivators actually took his servants, assaulted one of them; killed another and stoned one of them as well.

He sent other servants, more than the first time and they did the same to them as they did to the others. Later he sent towards them his son, saying, "They will respect my son." But the cultivators having seen the son, said to themselves, "This is the heir; let's kill him and have his inheritance," and they took him and threw him outside the vineyard and they killed him.

The good harvest
of fruit from God's creation
is owed to Him.
Loyally His people
aspire to be carriers of our Lord's Love.
The anti-Christ's loathsome system
of control and tribulation
is resolutely resisted.
Abhorring evil
the persecuted respond
to blatant savagery
with courage and self-restraint.
Nothing
will end our faith
in God and humanity.
The time is anticipated
when our heinous and belligerent enemy
will no longer cause cruel calamity.
Those who have been persecuted
because of their justness are happy
as The Kingdom of Heaven is theirs.

If the world hates you, know that it has hated me before it hated you.

John ~ chapter 15 verse 18

Love your enemies and pray for those persecuting you.

Matthew ~ chapter 5 verse 44

I came from the Father into the world.

John ~ chapter 16 verse 28

It is the Father remaining in union with me who is doing His work.

John ~ chapter 14 verse 10

And so Jesus went on to say to the Jews that had believed him, "If you remain in my Word you are really my disciples, and you will know the Truth and the Truth will set you free."

John ~ chapter 8 verse 31

Therefore, whenever you are praying, say,

Our Father in the Heavens;
let Your name be kept sacred.
Let your Kingdom come,
let Your Will take place
as it does in Heaven
also upon Earth.
Give us today,
the bread we need.
Forgive us our debts,
as we forgive the debts
of everyone owing to us.
Do not bring us into temptation
but rescue us from the wicked one.

Matthew ~ chapter 6 verse 9
Luke ~ chapter 11 verse 2

Whoever does not Love me does not keep my words.

John ~ chapter 14 verse 24

www.ingramcontent.com/pod-product-compliance
Lightning Source LLC
LaVergne TN
LVHW041710060526
838201LV00043B/669